I0081100

MODERN SPIRITUAL WARFARE

WARFARE

Then vs Now

CHRISTOPHER A. MOORE

LOVE CLONES
publishing

Love Clones Publishing
www.lcpublishing.net

Copyright © 2016 by Christopher A. Moore. All rights reserved. This book or any portion thereof may not be reproduced or used in any manner whatsoever without the express written permission of the publisher except for the use of brief quotations in a book review.

Printed in the United States of America

First Printing, 2016

ISBN: 978-0692615300

King James Version Scripture quotations marked "KJV" are taken from the Holy Bible, King James Version (Public Domain).

New King James Version Scripture quotations marked "NKJV" are taken from the New King James Version. Copyright © 1982 by Thomas Nelson, Inc. Used by permission. All rights reserved.

Publishers:
Love Clones Publishing
Dallas, TX 75205
www.lcpublishing.net

TABLE OF CONTENTS

FOREWORD

I have known Overseer Christopher Moore for over twenty years. I have seen his life in ministry develop and mature into one of Camden County's most prolific speakers and visionary of our day.

His insight in the Word has challenged seasoned Elders in the Body of Christ to rethink their theology and move forward with God.

He has a timely anointing to truly walk as one of the sons of Issachar. In this great book, "Modern Spiritual Warfare, Then Verses Now", he challenges mature warriors to take another look at the way warfare is being fought in this present generation. You will appreciate how he embraces the past but ushers us into the future warfare of today.

Overseer Moore's book is indeed an eye opener to the devices that we innocently celebrate. Spiritually, they are taking our youth by storm. From cell phones to IPads, from IPhone to Facebook, from Twitter to Snapchat and to the entire move of modern technology, he offers strategies to assist and educate God's people so that they can be better equipped for warfare.

I challenge every believer, especially leaders, to read this book for your knowledge and to remain in tune with the new devices of satan that Paul clearly admonished us that we are not to be ignorant of.

Finally, if you are a warrior in the Body of Christ, you will need the tools provided in this book to become a more efficient warrior of our day.

Sincerely submitted,
Dr. Erta Livingston, Jr.

INTRODUCTION

Spiritual warfare, what do those words mean to you?

Spiritual warfare has been around for ages. The first indication of such activity was when the fallen angels fell from Heaven onto the earth with satan (Isaiah 14:12-14). There is a great deal of information available when it comes to the subject of spiritual warfare and demonic activities such as witchcraft, black & white magic, voodoo, Ouija board, tarot cards, psychic, palm reading, demonic astrologers, and clairvoyance, etc. Just like medications there are new names being used for the same types of demonic activity.

There has been a vast array of books, articles, and documented cases of spiritual warfare, demonic activity and possession. From the famous documented Salem witch trials to the Hollywood depiction of demonic warfare in the movie "The Exorcist" when a Catholic Priest performed an exorcism on the main character in the movie.

Demonic activity is prevalent in the modern day church and because of this there has been several methods of dealing with such demonic undertakings.

Now, if you were raised in the "traditional church" like I was, when you consider spiritual warfare, you have images in your head of witches, warlocks, demons, and imps. You may even recall attacks that you or others may have experienced at the hands of the Believer's enemy whom we call the devil. You may be very familiar with the term "being under a spiritual attack".

The topic of spiritual warfare can no longer be approached in the same way that it was when our grandmothers were young, saved, and on fire for God because things are different now. The way we live has changed due to the heightened development of technology. Just think we don't listen to music on records and 45's like our grandparents did, we have Ipods, phones, and live streaming, etc.

The hardest transition for people in the 60's was going from records and 45's to 8 track tapes. Then in the 70's there was a transition from 8 track tapes to cassette tapes. Then there was a transition from cassette tapes to the more current way we listen to music, which is through CD's. The transition was made and we enjoyed a better quality of sound and convenience. Then the transition went from CD's to something known as music player or mp3 player, which really didn't last long due to technological advancements.

A major technology giant had an idea that we could listen to music with our cellphones, which is another major technological advancement in and of itself.

In the 21st century the way we listen to music is still changing and becoming more progressive. We can listen to an entire album or a single with something as simple as a cellphone. We don't have to wait until we are home to play a record on the record player anymore. We now have modern devices that are more convenient.

As technology advances and changes the world, the only thing that is consistent is that spiritual warfare is still very real. Now let me make this clear. I believe that witches, warlocks, black magic, voodoo etc. is still alive and occurring in the world today and in the body of the church as a whole. I am in no way saying that those types of forces have retired and are no longer in operation. However we have to now bring our attention to the modern and updated version of how the enemy is operating in order to combat the devil on the level that he is functioning today. You see we can no longer deal with the devil in the VCR warfare when we're in the age of Blue Ray discs!

I know you're asking how I am qualified to tackle a topic of this magnitude and bridge the gap between the old pattern of spiritual warfare and what I will present to you now as the NEW Modern PATTERN of spiritual warfare. I was born and raised in the old-style apostolic church. I have witnessed bodies levitating from the ground and demons calling out the dead parents of those that were trying to cast the spirit out. I've seen witches that weigh 140lbs lift benches and literally throw men off of them who were trying to hold them down. I have seen less of this pattern in our local church and the use of more crafty devices used by the enemy to enslave the minds of the Kingdom of God, specifically our youth.

I want you to take everything that you've ever heard about spiritual warfare and place it in the back of your mind. I do not want you to get rid of it but what I want you to do is use it as the beginning for where we are going. I am not saying tear down all of your belief systems concerning spiritual warfare but we cannot continue to combat the enemy with outdated information, strategies, tools, and technologies. The only thing that I ask is for you to have an open new mind.

What is Modern Spiritual Warfare?

Modern spiritual warfare, what does that mean?
What does that mean for us today?

Ponder this when was the last time you wrote a four page letter with pen and paper put it in an envelope, put a stamp on it and sent it to someone? It has been a long time right? It sure has been for me.

Consider when was the last time you posted to someone's Facebook page or sent them a message? In fact when was the last time you sent someone a text?

Technology has given you the ability to contact people. Where you would have had to spend money to send a letter, you can now text someone or you can inbox someone on Facebook.

Our older aunts, uncles and grandmothers are getting Facebook now because they see the benefit of being connected to their family instantaneously.

So let's say that we had a combat mission and that mission was to intercept any letters that came by way of traditional mail.

If we spent all of our time intercepting letters that were sent to people by regular mail we would find ourselves dealing with the penal system because it's one of the few places where letters are a major form of communication. However, in everyday life we can't put the focus of our mission on just letters when the enemy now has an upgraded method of sending information, i.e. via social media. He is no longer using the old spiritual pattern of standard mail. If we become distracted by an old method, the enemy can then infiltrate the Kingdom by way of newer technology. Thus it appears we are not using the same tools and level of force to combat him.

The way to strategically combat this in the spirit realm, we're going to have to "intercept" the emails that he's sending as well as the Facebook inboxes, twitter tweets, and Instagram images. If we're going to be a barrier between what was and what is, our minds have to change because technology has changed.

WITCHES, WARLOCKS, TIGERS, & BEARS OH MY!

In the church, focus is on one type of spiritual warfare, which is dealing with demons only. Witches, warlocks, tigers, and bears oh my! We've focused on that one opportunity of dealing with demons one on one. I present to you that we have been dealing with spiritual warfare from an old pattern, which is not based on scripture.

Think about a police officer that carries a weapon. There are some police officers that go their entire career and never have to draw their weapon to shoot anyone. While there are some officers, who graduate straight out of the academy and within their first year have to use their weapon. What if a police officer woke up every morning and their mindset was to go out and use only certain parts of their training. In this example we will say that the officer is only using the discharge of weapons training that they received from the Police Academy. What if that is the only opportunity they are looking for?

If so, then people breaking in cars, houses, committing other types of theft and rape will go unchecked because the police officer would only be looking for the opportunity to discharge his weapon, catching an assailant in the act.

That is what happens with spiritual warfare, in some churches today. We are looking for those opportunities of walking into rooms ready to cast out demons and spirits. Even though we are trained to cast out demons, the truth of the matter is you may live your entire Kingdom experience and never have to cast out a devil. I am going to change your mindset about the traditional way we have been dealing with casting out demons and what spiritual warfare is.

POWER OR NAH?

Mark 5:1-13 (NKJV) A Demon-Possessed Man Healed
Then they came to the other side of the sea, to the country of the Gadarenes. 2 And when He had come out of the boat, immediately there met Him out of the tombs a man with an unclean spirit, 3 who had his dwelling among the tombs; and no one could bind him, not even with chains, 4 because he had often been bound with shackles and chains. And the chains had been pulled apart by him, and the shackles broken in pieces; neither could anyone tame him. 5 And always, night and day, he was in the mountains and in the tombs, crying out and cutting himself with stones. 6 When he saw Jesus from afar, he ran and worshiped Him. 7 And he cried out with a loud voice and said, "What have I to do with You, Jesus, Son of the Most High God? I implore you by God that You do not torment me." 8 For He said to him, "Come out of the man, unclean spirit!" 9 Then He asked him, "What is your name?" And he answered, saying, "My name is Legion; for we are many." 10 Also he begged Him earnestly that He would not send them out of the country. 11 "Blessed are you when they revile and persecute you, and say all kinds of evil against you falsely for My sake. 12 Rejoice and be exceedingly glad, for great is your reward in heaven, for so they persecuted the prophets who were before you.13 "You are the salt of the earth; but if the salt loses its flavor, how shall it be seasoned? It is then good for nothing but to be thrown out and trampled underfoot by men.

In order to change your mind set about the traditional ways we've been dealing with casting out demons and spiritual warfare, I would like for you to take a look at the scriptural passage we tend to teach from concerning casting out demons. The first thing that I want you to notice is that Jesus did not walk around looking for demons. Aren't we to pattern ourselves after Jesus?

Greater works shall we do! Jesus never ran after demons. You will never find, in the Word where Jesus said, "come out in the name of me." You will never find in the Bible where He was on the floor rolling around with demons. You'll never see in the Word where He was running around being theatrical and daring demons saying "don't come for me unless I call for you" or things like "I'm ready for demons" or saying that He was a demon buster or "I don't play". He never said that He was anointed to cast out demons nor did He try to show off in front of the disciples. He knew who He was and the disciples knew who He was. The power that He operated in was enough.

The Bible clearly says when Jesus showed up the demons immediately manifested and reported to the highest power present and worshipped Him. When you walk in true power you don't have to search for demons. If in the presence of demons they should come subject to the authority of God that lives on the inside of you. It should be clear that everyone that comes to worship is not a Believer. Are we clear that demons, witches and warlocks come to our churches not delivered, but when we have the power that we are supposed to function in they will become subject to our authority.

STOP TALKING TO DEMONS!

The next thing I want to tackle is talking to demon. I want to tear down another broken pattern that is being used in error when it comes to spiritual warfare. There are many that operate in spiritual warfare that are asking demons their name, how long have they been possessing someone, how did they get there, what did they cause a person to do and more. They engage in a full-blown conversation with the enemy. Sort of like an interrogation session in the house of God, giving the enemy exactly what he wants which is a show and to be seen in God's presence.

Remember what got the devil in trouble originally; he loves nothing more than to be in God's house and to be worshipped. I was taught and I believe that you do not give the devil any room. You tell him to SHUT UP and become subject to the Power of GOD! The devil has two choices to come out or shut up. Those that believe that we should practice speaking to demons are based on the fact that Jesus spoke but let's look at it a little closer.

Notice the demonic force came immediately to Jesus and began worshipping Him and there was no intention of him trying to commit any bodily harm to Jesus or the disciples. However, in some churches demons do not come in peace. In worship they come to cause trouble and often times, wanting to cause bodily harm and distracting the service, which takes our attention away from the worship of God.

Furthermore, that the demon came begging Jesus not to be cast out however today demons say that they are not coming out.

I am not saying that if you speak to demons and have power that it will not come out. However, I come to you as Paul said to us in the New Testament let me show you a more excellent way.

1St Corinthian 12:31 (NKJV) But earnestly desire the best gifts. And yet I show you a more excellent way.

RECEIVING "THE POWER"

Acts 2: 1-4 (NKJV)
When the Day of Pentecost had fully come, they were all with one accord in one place. 2 And suddenly there came a sound from heaven, as of a rushing mighty wind, and it filled the whole house where they were sitting. 3 Then there appeared to them divided tongues, as of fire, and one sat upon each of them. 4 And they were all filled with the Holy Spirit and began to speak with other tongues, as the Spirit gave them utterance.

Now remember that open mind thing that we spoke of earlier? Now is the time to activate it. I want to share with you a personal testimony. I received the gift of the Holy Ghost when I was thirteen years old calling on the name of Jesus for eight months every Tuesday night for two hours straight. I foamed at the mouth or as we said back then "purged". I was thirteen years old and I was tired of going to church every Tuesday yelling Jesus, screaming at the top of my lungs, yelling for a Jesus who I was told had power and that He would give it to me if I asked for it. At thirteen, I was taught about Jesus and I saw how others received the power that Jesus had. I knew and heard about Him but had not really believed in the POWER of His name for a new tongue.

I read in the Bible how the people waited for a power in what was called the upper room for approximately 10-15 days (Acts 2: 1-4).

However, I also read that after they received the power, which is the same power that Believers have today, in Acts 8, they no longer had to wait for that power nor did the Apostles teach the Believers that came after them that in order to receive the same power they had to wait for it. I remember it like it was yesterday. On the way to church I told my mother that I would receive the Holy Ghost that night. Once we arrived at church it was not even two minutes of being on the altar that I received the precious gift of the Holy Ghost. I believe that it took a short time for me to receive the Holy Ghost because I had a made up mind and I was ready to receive what was already given to me, which was the same power that those in the Bible received before me.

They believed in the power that they possessed and so did I. They laid hands on Believers and they were immediately filled with the Holy Ghost and this is the more excellent way or the greater works than these, Jesus spoke of.

Once again people of God I am not suggesting that if you speak to demons or wrestle with them that they won't leave or be cast out but what I am saying is that once you come into the real and full understanding of the power that you possess, you have an obligation to embrace present truth. Even today you can use a horse and buggy to go to Walmart however the more excellent way would be to drive your car!

THE TRUTH ABOUT THE MUSTARD SEED

I want to tear down another old pattern of belief concerning spiritual warfare in the body of Christ. The pattern is that you have to be a member of the Five-Fold Ministry or hold a title in the church, be super deep, or go through some sort of demonic warfare training. The biggest lie of all is that your life must be *perfect* in order to confront an immediate opposing threat of a demonic force.

Allow me to release a secret that might get my apostolic card pulled. The truth is some leaders want, need, and financially insist on you to depend on them to deal with demonic forces that are after you, your children, and your entire household. Yet the truth of the matter is, if you are a Believer you have the power to make the devil back up off of you and yours.

Let's look at verse Matthew 17:19-20
19 Then the disciples came to Jesus privately and said, "Why could we not cast it out?" 20 So Jesus said to them, "Because of your unbelief; for assuredly, I say to you, if you have faith as a mustard seed, you will say to this mountain, 'Move from here to there,' and it will move; and nothing will be impossible for you.

The disciples asked why could we not cast the demon out. Notice what Jesus did not say. He did not say that you did not have enough power or that you didn't have enough training. Keep in my mind that they were disciples and had not been elevated to the office of the Apostle. He simply said "because of your unbelief."

It is the exact same reason why many go to church and have experienced the power of Jesus and still do not believe in the power of His name. Notice, Jesus asked these same disciples in Matthew 16:13 "Who do men say that I am?" Only Peter declares, "Thou art the Christ the Son of the living God." Jesus replies, "Upon this rock I build my church." What was the Rock? The rock was belief in Christ!

With that in mind let's now read verse 20

*²⁰ And Jesus said unto them, Because of your unbelief: for verily I say unto you, if ye have faith as a **grain of mustard seed**, ye shall say unto this mountain, Remove hence to yonder place; and it shall remove; and nothing shall be impossible unto you.*

This verse and the analogy of the mustard seed faith, has widely been used out of context. We have applied the mustard seed faith to prosperity and individual desires. However, when you look at the mustard seed faith and connect it to the text, it should be applied to your ability to cast out or remove any demon of a mountain size. While we're here, as they

CHRISTOPHER A. MOORE

say in the south let me give you this for free. The devil is not bound to hell. So when casting out a demonic host, do not shout I send you to the pit of hell because you're sending him to a place that he is legally not allowed to go to yet and he couldn't go there if he wanted to.

When casting out a demonic host you command him to be removed to yonder, dark and dry places of the earth. Those that live in rural areas know that when your city or county is being cultivated there are usually large amounts of areas that were woods for decades in desolate places. When these areas are being cut down for construction or cultivation it is important that you cover your house and your property under the blood of Jesus.

Let's look at verse 21

²¹ *Howbeit this kind goeth not out but by prayer and fasting.*

Notice what Jesus is saying, a mountain-sized demon will come out if you strengthen your belief in God. Jesus continues to exhort on prayer and fasting. Prayer and fasting are the two foundational tools that connect the Believers to God and keeps us forever connected to God's presence. It is impossible to pray and fast and your belief in God remains smaller than a mustard seed.

JESUS! ACCESS GRANTED

Acts 19:6-17 (KJV)

6 And when Paul had laid his hands upon them, the Holy Ghost came on them; and they spake with tongues, and prophesied. 7 And all the men were about twelve. 8 And he went into the synagogue, and spake boldly for the space of three months, disputing and persuading the things concerning the kingdom of God. 9 But when divers were hardened, and believed not, but spake evil of that way before the multitude, he departed from them, and separated the disciples, disputing daily in the school of one Tyrannus. 10 And this continued by the space of two years; so that all they which dwelt in Asia heard the word of the Lord Jesus, both Jews and Greeks. 11 And God wrought special miracles by the hands of Paul: 12 So that from his body were brought unto the sick handkerchiefs or aprons, and the diseases departed from them, and the evil spirits went out of them. 13 Then certain of the vagabond Jews, exorcists, took upon them to call over them which had evil spirits the name of the LORD Jesus, saying, we adjure you by Jesus whom Paul preacheth. 14 And there were seven sons of one Sceva, a Jew, and chief of the priests, which did so. 15 And the evil spirit answered and said, Jesus I know, and Paul I know; but who are ye? 16 And the man in whom the evil spirit was leaped on them, and overcame them, and prevailed against them, so that they fled out of that house naked and wounded. 17 And this was known to all the Jews and Greeks also dwelling at Ephesus; and fear fell on them all, and the name of the Lord Jesus was magnified.

This is a great place to discuss the use of the name of Jesus. Some use certain scriptures to support the belief that you should not use JESUS' name unless you're the elite. Those that are Believers should use the name of Jesus. So what qualifies you to become a Believer? Let's see, *Romans 10:9-10 says that ⁹that if thou shalt confess with thy mouth the Lord Jesus, and shalt believe in thine heart that God hath raised him from the dead, thou shalt be saved. ¹⁰For with the heart man believeth unto righteousness; and with the mouth confession is made unto salvation.*

The Word of God says, when you confess with your mouth and believe in your heart that God raised Jesus from the dead you will be saved. Once you do that you are considered a Believer, which gives you the right to use His name. Please note that this is a two-step process because there are people who confess with their mouth but never believe in their heart. I can say I love you with my mouth but if I don't believe it with my heart then my actions will never line up with what I said. This is the reason why we built these "rules". There have been people in our churches that called on Jesus and could not handle demons. Why, because they are not Believers. If you're calling Jesus and nothing is happening and nothing is moving, you have to check your salvation and your relationship with God because when your relationship with God is unquestionable and you are a Believer all you have to say is in the name of Jesus.

Unfortunately, you have heard over and over that if you have not gone through elite spiritual warfare training, demons will tear your behind up, like the Seven Sons of Sceva. The problem with that is we become too spooky because we think that casting out demons is deep.

The first thing that I will like to show you about the scripture is this. Paul cast out demons and he spent two years healing and teaching the full Gospel of Jesus Christ. His focus was not demonology. He cast out spirits as needed. Paul who is doing the will of the Lord cast out demons but doesn't make it his focus. Jesus never made casting out demons His focus. He showed up and things became subject. We've already discussed earlier when Jesus told the disciples in Matthew if you have mustard seed size faith every demon in hell has to come subject.

Let me make this clear, we must cast out demons. However, when we our ministries are totally concentrated only with demonology we remove ourselves from operating in the fullness of what we have access to. We must teach Believers not to go looking for demons. However, if Believers are confronted or find themselves in the presence of demonic activity they have the ability through the name of Jesus to defend **themselves** against spiritual warfare. It is incorrect to use these Scriptures as a basis that they should be afraid to use the name of Jesus unless they have met their individual church ministry's standards.

I also want to take a look closely at **who** was stripped naked. They were unbelievers; they were not filled with the Holy Ghost.

Acts 19:13 (KJV) <u>*then certain of the vagabond Jews, exorcists,*</u> *took upon them to call over them which had evil spirits the name of the LORD Jesus, saying, we adjure you by Jesus whom Paul preacheth. [14] And there were seven sons of one Sceva, a Jew, and chief of the priests, which did so.*

The Bible speaks specifically about *certain vagabonds Jews and exorcists.* First let's tackle what vagabond Jew is. The Vagabond Jews were people who wandered with no place to live and without regular work, people who wandered from place to place and lived by means of begging. They also went from town to town casting out evil spirits and this time they thought they could do it in the name of "Paul's Jesus".

The Bible also says the exorcists also tried to use "Paul's Jesus". An Exorcist is a person who is believed to be able to cast out the devil or other demons.

To use these verses as means of telling **Believers** that they must be careful when using Jesus' name is incorrect. If you are a Believer you have full authority to use Jesus' name and you have access to everything that He has.

When you use the name of Jesus the devil does not hear you but in actuality the devil hears the voice of the hosts of heaven and has no choice but to become subject.

Let's be reminded of *Matthew 11:11-12*

*11 Verily I say unto you, among them that are born of women there hath not risen a greater than John the Baptist: notwithstanding he that is **least in the kingdom of heaven** is greater than he. 12 And from the days of John the Baptist until now the kingdom of heaven suffereth violence, and the violent take it by force.*

Notice that Scripture says **least** in the kingdom of heaven. Also notice verse 12 says "the kingdom of heaven suffered violence," who else causes violence in the kingdom of heaven except the devil and his demonic forces. More importantly pay attention to *who* has the ability to take it by force, *He who is least in the kingdom.*

The Old Testament prophets prophesied that Jesus was to come. Jesus said that John the Baptist was greater than them because he declared that Jesus is here. The least Believer in the kingdom of heaven is greater than them all because Jesus lives in us; therefore I proclaim again that true Believers have access to use Jesus's name when casting out devils. Don't make it spooky and get to deep casting out demons. It is simply believing and using the name. It is the right of the Believer!

The bottom line is this. He paid the price for you to use His name! **SO USE IT!!!**

MODERN SPIRITUAL WARFARE

In this chapter we will discuss the new pattern of spiritual warfare because again the devil is not using regular and standard mail letters anymore. The devil is not using witches and warlocks and the things that we have focused on thus far. Think about this, if the devil didn't use witches and warlocks to try to come against Jesus, why do we still think that is his pattern for today. Please don't get me wrong; he can always call on a witch. He can always pull on a warlock. Those are old patterns he can reach back and resort to at any given time but those are not his first tools anymore.

Let's examine what warfare is. If America and China went into battle right now they would not meet on a battlefield like Gettysburg with America on one side and China on the other and then clash in the middle of the field. We don't fight like that anymore. Can you imagine if I went to war right now in Afghanistan with a musket? Could you imagine if a police officer had on his uniform and got out of his car and responded to a shots fired call with a sword and everyone else had guns?

There was once a time when the sword was the best weapon in the land. There was also a time, when a musket was the best gun available. That was the technology of that day. However, if you're coming to the battle today with a musket and someone else has a

Glock, you're as good as dead. I'll prove it to you even more. Think about a 6 ft. 5 in. man who weighed 325lbs. Now think about a six-year-old boy. Think about and picture how big, strong and tall this man is with a sword in his hand and the little boy with a Glock in his hand. Who is going to win? The six-year-old is going to win. That's what's happening in our church. Spirits and demons weaker and lesser than us are winning because we are showing up with an old pattern and outdated weapons. Therefore, let me assist you in changing your mindset when you're dealing with modern spiritual warfare against an enemy who is working with a more modern and established way of defeating you. We can no longer keep old patterns of thinking things have to be done the same way.

We must have quick and appropriate responses because the world changes. In warfare, position changes. Our warfare has changed and if we're going to win we can't deal with it based on old patterns, dogmas, and church rituals that can't be supported in the Word.

A set of rules with an old pattern works in controlled environments. Habitual deviation from understanding that things change is going to always bring you failure. Some people are habitual in the fact that they refuse to change their mind set about spiritual warfare and they always show up with a knife to a gunfight.

ESTIMATING THE BEHAVIOR OF MY ENEMY

Estimating the behavior of my enemy means that I have to gauge my enemy to see what they are going to do next. Based on what I discover I must be able to counter it with an appropriate response. If I'm not paying attention to my enemy and he moves to another place and I don't change my location it will ultimately cause defeat. I must observe my enemy to see what he is doing now to determine what he is going to do next which will tell me what his new course of actions would be; ultimately helping me to estimate his intentions so that I can be prepared for any move that he tries to make.

Ephesians 6:11-12
11 Put on the whole armour of God that ye may be able to stand against the wiles of the devil. 12 For we wrestle not against flesh and blood, but against principalities, against powers, against the rulers of the darkness of this world, against spiritual wickedness in high places.

There are demons and demonic spirits working and lurking. Demonic warfare is real. Ephesians 6:11 reads, *put on the whole armour of God, that ye may be able to stand against the wiles of the devil. It continues to read, for we wrestle not against flesh and blood, but against principalities, against powers, against the rulers of the darkness of this world, against spiritual wickedness in high places.*

There are demons over our heads that are looking down on our behaviors and seeing what they can do to strategically make us fall. So while we're looking at each other, they are looking at us. Do you not know that as anointed, powerful, and charismatic as some people are, they still have weaknesses. If you follow them for a short period of time you might just see something that exposes one of their weakness. If people watch you long enough, knowingly or unknowingly you can expose your weaknesses.

Therefore, while we're fighting each other, the enemy is in the heavenlies looking down on us, but he is not, looking down on us saying, 'I'm going to conjure up a witch or warlock to deal with the Body of Christ'. Think about this, when was the last time you dealt with a full fledge witch or warlock where you knew for a fact that they were 100% dealing with witchcraft? The truth of the matter is, they are in place but not his first choice at this time. When was the last time you felt lonely, when is the last time you felt vulnerable, these are the tools that the devil is using.

Principalities of This Age:

I need you to understand there is a ranking system in the devil's kingdom. The principalities are the highest. The authorities are next and then the world rulers. It is the job of the world rulers to scope out the tools and technology of today, report it back to either the authorities or the principalities in order to bring people into bondage. It compares to the levels of authority to a police officer that works for a precinct. Have you seen the Chief of Police of your city riding around in a patrol car? Almost never. When was the last time you saw one of his officers riding around patrolling and enforcing traffic violations? All the time. It is the job of the police officer to report back what is happening on the street to a higher office. The ultimate goal is getting to the Chief so that a plan can be put into place as to how to combat what is happening on the street.

The Chief will then send back down strategies to be executed on the street. The witches, the warlocks and the heavy spiritual warfare that we have been focusing on, is there, but it is the world rulers amongst us trying to figure out how they can trap the people of God. So the devil uses everything that he can on the street. Those that are at the bottom, say 'no it's not letters anymore it's the Internet'. Those on the bottom say, 'nope you don't have to send witches to their churches anymore, what you can do is get animosity amongst them by their Facebook stalking and taking things out of proportion'. The world rulers are using the modern things of today.

Let's go a little deeper.

If I want to change a people, one of the greatest ways is to change the mindset of the woman. The devil is after mothers because if he changes the mother's mind then he'll change the children's mind. The truth of the matter is men are strong but at the end of the day everyone in the house does what "mama" wants. So we must change our mind. So we must shift instead of looking at an old mentality. We have to make a modern shift. What is the word modern; let's look at it.

I need you to get this because the devil is getting us by tearing up our children's mind. He's getting in our mind through modern methods. **Modern** means, *of or relating the present or recent times as oppose to the remote past. Of or relating to a recently developed style technique or technology, thus characteristics of present day art or music, literature and architecture.* The devil has the ability to take whatever is present of this current day and use it to alter the mindset of that generation. I call this Modern Spiritual Warfare.

II Corinthians 10:3
3 For though we walk in the flesh, we do not war after the flesh: 4 (For the weapons of our warfare are not carnal, but mighty through God to the pulling down of strong holds;) 5 Casting down imaginations, and every high thing that exalteth itself against the knowledge of God, and bringing into captivity every thought to the obedience of Christ;

Modern spiritual warfare is what the enemy is using to change our **imagination**. What is imagination? It is *the ability to form mental images of* *things that are not present to the sense or considered to be real.*

If I can change your mind to get you hyped up on things that are not real then you will want it and do anything in order to have it, casting down your desire to have what is not real. The devil is not coming the old way.

When thoughts and ideas increase and are left unchecked or redirected by modern spiritual awareness it will increase and change mindsets of people.

TYPES OF MODERN SPIRITUAL WARFARE

Modern Spiritual Warfare- Dancing

For those who can remember, the washing machine dance back in the 60's was forbidden. That dance was classified as a provocative and seductive dance. I present that the devil was changing his tactic of warfare then. This particular form of dancing increased from the washing machine to the bump in the 70's. Then in the 80's, women for the first time ever, were gyrating and bending over shaking their behinds back and forth without needing a male partner. All of this was done while men watched and cheered them on. The day of asking a woman to dance was laid to rest and a new modern form of dancing was birthed. Men and women alike are extremely comfortable gyrating and exposing themselves in front of mass audiences while being recorded and being shared around the world for the masses to see, share and like on sites such as Facebook or Tweeter. That has all lead into what is now known as Twerking. Again this is what I mean by modern spiritual warfare.

Can you see, when the mindset is changed the culture is changed and the expectations and the quality of life is minimized. In the 60's our grandmothers would do the wash machine, but they still desired to be married and if not married there was a demand of some sort of commitment. Now since the culture has changed some women today don't desire marriage. Deeper than that, back in the day, sleeping with a man for money was classified as prostitution or some more unsavory words that I will not use.

The expectations and the quality of life are minimized and are now viewed as prostitution rather than something that is accepted and applauded. The terminology that is used is, "It ain't trickin' if you got it." What the devil has now done is changed the imagination of women where now they feel good about something that is wrong as long as the right price is on the table.

The last time I checked, anytime you pay a woman for sex is prostitution. But since the church still has the washing machine mindset we don't have the proper response or the appropriate plan of action. We have found ourselves unequipped to deal with this new generation of "twerkers."

Modern Spiritual Warfare-Automobiles

Do you remember the old school Cadillac or maybe even the old '65 Ford Mustang? The men of that time would work all week and even some overtime in order to purchase these vehicles. When someone could not purchase a brand new car they would have an old one in the shed and after working all week they would spend time on the weekend fixing on it slowly until it was just right. At some point there was a shift from this mindset to the mindset of having the same fancy cars however, with no work ethic. Now the term of "quick money" has come into play. No one wants to make an honest pay. Day in and day out or work overtime anymore like our fathers did. Young men now want what they want and they want it now and they are willing to get it by any means.

The second culture shift was with the image of fame. Do you remember when hip-hop came into play with Kurtis Blow, Big Daddy Kane, and Kool Moe Dee? They were flashy. They had jewelry, clothing, and women. This was what young boys at the time called the life. This was also the beginning of the crack cocaine era. Crack cocaine gave young men a way to get what they wanted, quick fast and in a hurry and without working all week to get it. A good solid work ethic began to be a thing of the past. Then the image shifted again and the West Coast developed what was soon to be called Gangsta Rap by NWA and now with this came along an invincible spirit and the young boys of that time thought they couldn't be stopped by anyone. They were talking about guns, violence, and had total disrespect for the police and authority. This new ideology spread rapidly throughout the country and almost every "hood" was adopting this new belief system that hip-hop leaders declared.

Modern Spiritual Warfare-Music

The third shift in hip-hop was female rap. The women of that time wanted men to know that they could do everything that the men were doing. Do you remember Roxane Shante, Mc Lyte, and Queen Latifah? Those were the female rappers of that time. They believed they were just as bad as the men and could even take over the world if they wanted to. The ideology of women was they didn't need men. They were just as strong as the men and only needed them for pleasure and entertainment.

This attitude began to put a wedge in the relationship of men and women therefore, breaking down the family structure, which was not God's original plan. Then there were the female rappers who were strong but thought that they were sexy. They wore skimpy costumes or beachwear, grinding all on the stage in videos. They were very comfortable doing this. They also wanted the world to see that they were in control of their own bodies and much in charge of how they used their bodies, which was for fame, fortune, and validation.

All of that has led up to what is happening now, which is a generation where any and everything goes. The devil has penetrated the minds through modern warfare to where what is not normal is the norm. There are songs where it is advocated for women to dance on a pole as long as she comes home to her man. A glorification of what is called making it rain. This is when men throw lots of money in the air causing women to dance not only provocative like the days of the washing machine but to a whole new level of promiscuity. This causes the spirit of perversion to be overlooked and viewed as cute and common entertainment, which takes me back to my first point that modern spiritual warfare is a battle of the imagination.

Subsequently, while the Church is walking around speaking in tongues and pulling down strongholds the devil is using modern spiritual warfare to change the minds of our youth. This is what they are imagining. Our boys want to be ballers and shot-callers. They want to be dope boys. They don't want regular girls or wives anymore. They want trap queens, which is a combination of all of those female rappers that we spoke about earlier with an elevated to a "live or die" mentality. Girls who not only associate and have sex with drug dealers, but are viewed as females who can be taught how to cook up crack and keep the crack house in tact even when the drug dealer is not present.

It has become all about the bling! This is modern spiritual warfare. The devil has made young people go after the bling. Going after the Kingdom or attending church services is not a desire. He has enticed many into choosing to be drug dealers and to chase after money and cars. The pursuit of this fast lifestyle will cause them to never seek after the Kingdom of God and His righteousness. The devil knows that if they get the Kingdom of God all these things will be added. These are the *imaginations* that the devil is using. Therefore, we should be focusing our attention on creating new and effective patterns that will combat the modern spiritual warfare that the enemy has been using.

Modern Spiritual Warfare- Gangs

There are a great number of young adults that are turning to gangs as a way of substituting the sense of being a part of a family. There is a gap between the younger generation and the church. The church has not progressed and has remained dogmatic in their beliefs and has not changed from the old patterns of spiritual warfare or the strong set of principles that worked for earlier generations. Thus, when young people come into our doors we are trying to cast out demons instead of trying to change their imaginations or mindset. What we have to do is change how they see the church and create an atmosphere of where they feel accepted no matter what or who they are. This is not to say that we will not as a church confront or deal with the demonic strongholds that is over their lives but what it does mean is that we will have more open invitations and open opportunities to bring true deliverance to those that are bound.

Modern Spiritual Warfare - Technology

Let's take a look into two more of the absolute greatest tools that the enemy is using in modern spiritual warfare through technology and social media.

Cellular Phones

It has been said that the cellular phone is man's greatest and worst invention. Cellular phones were invented for one reason and that reason was convenience. The cell phone is a key that opens portals that some have gotten lost in and have built new realities in a superficial world. The cell phone has gone from being a device that only calls people to now being a tool that is a computer in your hand. Because of this, it is a mobile connector to social media wherever you go. Everyone has one or everyone desires one and most people upgrade their phones religiously.

Social Media

Social Media is like a vehicle. You can drive it to church or to the liquor store. Sadly, social media is a form of transportation that is being used to drive many people away from God. Social Media is a world within itself. The truth of the matter is that you can live an entire life through these media platforms without ever having to go outside. Social media has become a tool that the devil is using where people will mask their depression and their fear of the world because they never have to leave the comfort of their home.

These same people experience weight gain, poor health, anxiety, and a host of other mental, physical, and psychological abnormalities. People are seeing images and videos of other people's lives and feel as if they cannot meet the standards of what they see. This leads to feelings of inadequacy, low self-esteem, depression, and rejection from what they have created and imagined in their own minds. This has been a contributor to the rise of suicide of both teens and adults.

Now let's look at different forms of Social Media.

Facebook

People have developed a false sense of friendship on Facebook. When we were growing up, your friends were actual people that you played with every day. If you got into a fight it took a few days of being alone and you made up because you realized that you had no one else to play with. Today, people have no problem with not building or valuing friendships because there are ten other people in their friend request waiting to be their "new friend".

Facebook has also incited divorce, fights, deaths and shootings, because people who would normally not say anything at all now become bold and express to the fullest what and how they feel.

Facebook has become the cause of many robberies and burglaries because people are so quick to post or "check in" their exact locations.

There is a hidden sin of Facebook that is often missed, and the devil is using it to shift the minds of not only sinners but also saints alike. It is a spirit of self-idolatry. We tend to think that idolatry is worshipping a graven image of a being, idea, or thing. However, idolatry is anything that you worship or give a greater amount of passion or concern to more than you do God. One can become consumed about having the perfect perception, picture, and images of themselves. If not careful the over exaggeration of one's own life can lead to self-idolatry. You now begin to seek the validation of others through Facebook likes. You crave attention that you're receiving through comments, and if it is not given to you your next course of action is to obtain it through lies, exaggeration, and manipulation all to obtain self-gratification.

The same can be done when one becomes overly infatuated with the lives of others. This is also a form of idolizing which is again substituting a graven image of a being, idea, or thing in the place of God. All of the above is hidden and goes unrecognized because you're being lured in by the daily gratification of being engaged and entertained on Facebook.

YouTube

The days of pay per view pornography is almost nonexistent. Pornography is so readily available to our youth that it has become very difficult for them not to be exposed to some level of impurity at ages younger than we encountered.

When I was a kid if my friends and I wanted to look at dirty magazines, it was a big deal. It meant that someone would have to steal an old one from his father's collection that he wouldn't readily miss and we would have to hide it under a mattress or in our tree house. Back then there were two major pornography magazines. The first one was Playboy and if your daddy was real nasty, he had Hustler.

Pornography was not available to us then like it is today. As we previously discussed everybody has a cellular phone. Unlike the days when we could monitor what they had access to on our home computers, they can now access YouTube with their cellular phones. Of course we know that some kids are directly and purposely logging onto YouTube to look at pornography, but for those who are typing in the wrong words, you will get a grand surprise. This may be viewed as soft porn to adults. For children who are seeing it for the first time, it introduces and opens them up to a whole new world that they are not ready for.

You see YouTube in advertisement zone and it operates on keywords that link several video topics with another. For example if you type in Spaulding basketball, you will not only get videos about the basketball itself but you will get videos and images about the NBA, Michael Jordan, LeBron James, and Steph Curry. Can you see how this works? You see you're getting the links to pornography, videos, and images and that may not have been your intention.

Thus, the devil is not operating in the old patterns of spiritual warfare. While we're trying to attack the devil with a playboy and hustler warfare approach, he has shifted and is using a new pattern of modern spiritual warfare through this form of social media. Unfortunately, while we're still looking under mattresses, the enemy is trapping your children in the phone that you purchased for your child to call you on after school.

Our enemy is using what he has available to him which is social media and we must do the same if we want to save our children.

Modern Spiritual Warfare - Television

Reality Television

In order to destroy a generation you would first have to change their mindset. In order to change their mindset one would have to attack and discredit whom they view as their leadership. Then you would infiltrate the home and detach the father from the family, which will force the mothers to become dependent on an outside source. Once the mother is preoccupied with the daily burdens of life it is easier to swoop in and change the mindset of the children through their imaginations and the images that they see.

The family composition, dynamics, and mindset are being changed every day through television. I remember like it was yesterday, my grandmother, aunt and I would watch what we called soap operas religiously. We were not watching to see what people had on or what new cars were being driven and by whom. We were watching strictly to see what drama the Abbott family and the Newman's were cooking up. The difference between television today and television a long time ago was that we knew that once Days of Our Lives was over we had to go back to OUR lives because that was our reality and what really mattered.

Today's television era has transformed and we have what is called reality television which is when people film their lives for entertainment purposes to be viewed on television.

The Life of the Bling

The Bible says that the love of money is the root of all evil (1 Timothy 6:10). The lust of the eye and the pride of life (1 John 2:16) is causing people to tune in to see their favorite celebrities and stars expose their lives on television for their enjoyment and pleasure. Being that this is viewed as reality it is causing people who are not celebrities to chase after a life that is not attainable based on their own existences. You have people that are on a minimum wage salary trying to live a six-figure life because they are watching someone else's reality unfold. They are under the impression that the same life is attainable which is true. However, the means in which they can have it may not be the means, behavior or the pattern that God has laid out for obtaining these very same things.

The Family Life

Reality TV is shaping the family composition. The family is no longer considered a husband, a wife and children, but we are seeing an overwhelming level of respect given to what is called a player. On the soap operas back in the day, there was always the traditional idea of family. The man on the soap opera had a wife and children. If he decided that he didn't want the woman anymore he would divorce her and married whom he wanted. I am NOT trying to give praise to divorce. However, it showed at the very least, children being born into a traditional structure. Nowadays on reality TV, the man has had several women who he has had multiple children with and he is considered as the good guy when he is able to get the mothers of all of his children to get along. Marriage is not the ultimate goal and has been replaced with verbal commitments that are easily broken at any given moment. Believe it or not Believers of God have taken on this mentality as a direct result of being distracted of God's plan for their life by the indulgence of reality TV.

Television and the Homosexual Agenda

Television is being used to desensitize the very Christian morals and the fabric of our faith by making us have sympathy for the characters and lifestyles that if were spoken in a normal conversation would be called sin. There are several political and immoral agendas that are being infused with a Christian theme or a really good plot. This causes Believers and non-believers to have conversations at the water cooler about characters on television that is meant ultimately to become a conversation about their own homes. I would like to explore what I believe is one of the biggest agendas of our time which is the homosexual agenda.

Let's say one of your children came to you and said that they were gay. As a Believer of Christ and as a parent you would still love him. I pray that you would not be like the old school church and ostracize your child. The next question that I would like to ask you is would you ever accept your child's lifestyle as a Godly and Biblically approved union. The answer should be absolutely NO!

You would love them but you would never accept their lifestyle. You would do everything in your power to try to convince them to marry the opposite sex. We can never accept a homosexual lifestyle because by accepting this particular lifestyle we are saying that the Bible is a lie.

In 2014-2015 almost every major television network produced shows that had a main character that was homosexual. These shows made both Believers of Christ and non-believers alike to be upset with any character that tried to convince the gay character that homosexuality was wrong. We saw this played out when mothers try to convince their sons that they are not homosexual and with fathers disapproving of their son's gay lifestyle. We even saw those in political office being praised and defended to the max of anyone that came against the gay union. Finally, we observed the embrace of homosexuals adopting children. This was all done for three reasons.

Emotional attachment: Anger

When watching television one can become emotionally attached to the characters. When the character is confronted about their lifestyle, in this particular incident homosexuality, it can cause you to exude anger toward any other character that tries to convince your character that being gay is wrong. The mission of this agenda is to make you become angry in real life with anyone who opposes homosexuality.

Emotional attachment: Sympathy

Being angry will cause you to become sympathetic to your character. Now once you're sympathetic to the character, the agenda is for it to spill over into your reality. This is how you will recognize you're being desensitized to what you know is wrong. Why, because if you have sympathy for your character you will find yourself slowly having sympathy towards the people in your lives. And with anything or anyone that you have sympathy toward you will allow them to get away with more than what they should.

Emotional Attachment: Politics

The final step in the homosexual agenda is to obtain your votes to make lawful changes on their behalf. Understand if we are emotionally attached to homosexual characters and you've become lenient and desensitized to the two points above then when you're at the voting poll you're not thinking about your Bible or what is morally right! You're thinking about your favorite characters and the people in your lives and your vote becomes an emotional one that is not biblically based on your Christian morals and belief. In your mind you have been convinced that although you may not agree with their lifestyle they deserve to have the same rights as you.

We can look at the Supreme Court same-sex marriage decision as an example of what I am saying. Although we the people did not vote, the decision was made to allow same sex to marry. I believe that it was a result of modern spiritual warfare. By using subliminal and direct images thoughts and ideas through television radio and social media.

DEMOLISHING STRONGHOLDS

What is a Stronghold?

A stronghold is a place that has been set up or fortified to strengthen itself against an attack so that it can protect itself.

What is an Imagination?

The faculty of imagining thus, forming mental images, new ideas, and concepts of external objects of what is not actually present to the senses.

Now that we have defined what a stronghold is and what the word imagination is we can move forward with explaining to you how the two work together.

A stronghold is a fortified place in the mind to make you want and desire what is not your present life; the wanting of things that aren't the will of God or to produce behaviors that are not conducive to the believer's way of life. If these thoughts are not brought under subjection they become thoughts and desires that will exalt themselves against the knowledge of God; leaving you willing to pursue those things at any cost. A stronghold is a place that has been set up or fortified to strengthen itself against an attack so that it can protect itself.

We emphasize our weapons are spiritual and not physical. Once we accept the thoughts, we carry out the deeds of our mind that are no longer in the obedience of Jesus Christ. Therefore a stronghold is *any thought* that is in opposition in the objectives of Jesus Christ.

When these thoughts have been embedded in our minds the devil then knows that he has an avenue where he can create a warfare smoke screen. Which means that if he can keep us thinking that spiritual warfare is only of the old pattern, if he can keep you dancing, speaking in tongues, and running after witches and warlocks, he then can use everything thing modern to kill steal and destroy you and you won't realize it until it is too late.

We have to understand that we have to pull down strongholds. As previously stated modern spiritual warfare is changing the mind and the imagination of one's thoughts. I present to you that the stronghold of today's warfare is not the old pattern of witches and warlocks but the stronghold that we are dealing with today is the stronghold of the mind.

In many charismatic churches we have been taught and have spent a lot of time walking around, screaming, using our arms pulling up and down as we shout in what we call prophetic gestures. This is what some are calling pulling down strongholds. I present to you that this prophetic gesture is an incorrect and old pattern that needs to be revised.

With the revelation that the stronghold is in the mind, lets' look at two things. The first thing that I want to bring to your attention is that a stronghold is built from the bottom to the top. Imagine a wall that is separating two dimensions. If you knocked the top portion of the wall down and the foundation still remained you have a strong structure. However, there is now a breach in the security and stability of the wall, which can be easily repaired and even rebuilt. If you destroy the foundation totally in order for that stronghold to exist again it will have to be rebuilt from the bottom up. Therefore, if we are going to do any prophetic physical gestures the new and corrected pattern should be pulling from the bottom up and not the other way around. You should pull down the stronghold in this manner in order to pull up the root so that any potential for growth is nonexistent.

The second thing is that since the stronghold is in the mind we should take authority and command the thoughts and minds of Believers to become subject to the will of God. We should verbally use the authority in our voice and speak into the atmosphere the change that we want to see. However, in order to do this, we have to begin by speaking in the way people talk everyday which will allow them to be able to identify their issues easily. You see people today may not understand what it means to come against witches and warlocks and they do not see themselves in those terms. Therefore, when they come to church and hear the old patterns of spiritual warfare there is neither conviction nor a changing of imaginations. When you explain the new pattern that comes against the spirit of pornography that on YouTube, the spirit of procrastination or adultery on Facebook and the spirit of lust that develops when looking at someone's Facebook pictures and then you secretly inbox them.

The point that I am trying to make is that when people hear the present things they can identify and struggle with through modern spiritual warfare it causes a shift in their imagination. They will say to themselves that this is me and I need to change; thus the door to *true* deliverance and modern spiritual warfare being birthed. Now, there is no struggle and no fight and we will see today the pattern that we saw with Jesus when dealing with the woman at the well. He did not use words that she may have rejected or shunned. He spoke in a language that caused her to examine herself, accept what he said, and not only was she immediately delivered, she became an evangelist and went back to the city and told people that may have been dealing with demonic activity in their own life to come see a man.

We have seen over the years an old pattern of spiritual warfare that I believe has been common practice in the church. This common practice of forced deliverance is what I call spiritual rape. Now don't get me wrong I am not saying that there aren't instances where we would have to force deliver because of demonic activity that's being disruptive or even worse violent but if we're honest most of demonic warfare that's being performed in churches is not from people that are having loud outburst but rather from leaders who have the ability to recognize and diagnose spirits. However, the person that is being delivered may not be ready for it.

Matthew 12:45
45 Then goeth he, and taketh with himself seven other spirits more wicked than himself, and they enter in and dwell there: and the last state of that man is worse than the first. Even so shall it be also unto this wicked generation.

The Bible declares that when a demon is cast out he walks the earth trying to find a place that he can rest however when he cannot find such place he returns to the home that he once lived and he then takes along seven other demons that are more powerful than himself.

We have forced deliverance on people that did not want it. When we see them again weeks or even months later their state is worse than before. For example, there may be someone that you know that has struggled with cigarette addiction. If deliverance has been forced on them and the stronghold of their mind has not been broken, this same person, will not only go back to smoking cigarettes but the chances of them progressing to doing other things such as marijuana or "Dirties" (a mixture of marijuana and cocaine), is possible. There may even be a progression of snorting cocaine, then possibly smoking crack cocaine. The modern warfare that the devil is using with our young people is to make them feel that the old pattern or terminology of being called a crack head or drug user can be replaced with more up to date names. No one wants be called a crack head so the enemy has taken crack, mixed with other drugs and have given it new names such as "Popping Molly's" or on the X (ecstasy). These drugs are in pill form, you don't have to snort or smoke them but you can take them with water or Alcohol, like a Tylenol. This new modern method of drugs makes them feel like they're not necessarily taking drugs but a pill to feel a little better about what they're doing. However, the result is the same.

It is statistically proven that both men and women will resort to prostitution and indulge in homosexual encounters and will perform robberies and many other unlawful activities all to support all of the above addictions. Therefore, it is important that we counteract the enemy by changing the mindset of the people by dealing with the stronghold of the mind. Later I will give you tools that will assist you in moving from being oppressed and possessed by the enemy to totally being delivered and free from the enemy and his devices.

Let me give you an example of how your mind will ultimately direct your feet. Imagine the testimony service when a person stands and testifies that they thank God from being delivered from going to the night club dancing, drinking and smoking out but when they sit down their BODY is at the church but their mind is truly wondering what is going on at the club and truthfully missing it. This person, if their mind does not get delivered, their feelings will ultimately carry their mind, feet and body back into the club where they will soon encounter the drinking and smoking again.

Consider this same testimony but when the person sits down the club may be in their thoughts but their mind is engaged into the worship service and they are anticipating a word from the Lord. Both bodies are at the church but whom do you say is truly delivered? The old pattern says as long as the person is physically in church and are seen doing churchy things then they must be delivered. The new pattern of modern spiritual warfare says that it is not only concerned about the new physical presence of being in church but also about being delivered both in mind and body.

I am not saying that you will not have inappropriate thoughts about worldly things or about your past. You must understand, unlike God, we do not have the ability to throw our sins into the sea of forgetfulness. Therefore we are fashioned to remember thoughts whether good, bad, or indifferent. The memory of thoughts we can't control but through deliverance we can control our response to our thoughts.

Many people say that the Lord delivered them from a mighty *terrible world* of sin. Let me be honest. Although I gave my life to the Lord at the age of 8 years old and started preaching at the age of 14, there was a time in my adult life where I veered from the truth and led a sinful life experiencing the world and all that it had to offer.

With this I discovered that some things were not terrible and actually at the time I *thought* was terrific. With that being said there were things that we did in the world that we liked doing. If you went to the club you did not go because it made you feel bad. Many went to the club to be entertained, relaxed and to possibly meet who you thought would perhaps become a future relationship or a hook up for that night. We did not go to the hotel with the mindset of having a bad experience. The list can go on and on but my point is this, there are memories of our past whether places or people that when we think of it/them, it does not bring a bad feeling until after we act upon them.

I believe that many of you feel the same way as I do. I didn't come to the Kingdom of God because I was what some would call busted and disgusted or because I had a lack of friends or social events to attend. I did not give my life to the Lord because I desired a woman, money, cars, or houses.

I had all of those things in the world and lacked nothing. The problem is even though I had all of those things it created a false sense of peace. Anything that does not have God as the center is an earthly possession. Although it gives temporary enjoyment it will lead to eternal damnation.

Therefore, it is natural that even after giving your life to the Lord that there will be times that your mind will have thoughts of the enjoyment of your past.

However, when the stronghold of your mind has been delivered and swept clean as the Bible declares, you will be able to fight against the wiles of the devil.

Furthermore, the Bible says that when the demon comes back after you've been swept clean he will go back and get seven other demons stronger than himself. When he comes back and finds out that it is clean a second time and see that you're about the Father's business he will depart from you. This is what James 4:7 means when it says submit yourselves therefore to God. Resist the devil, and he will flee from you.

I believe that this is where we stopped in our thought process of deliverance but let me put this in your mind for thought. If you were up for an inspection for your home and you swept clean all of the dirt, will that dirt ever come back? The answer is yes. In order for your house to stay clean, you will have to continually clean it. That is why I am presenting to you that we must renew our mind daily; so when there's a surprise inspection of the enemy he will never find your house (mind) un-swept.

Thus, when the things of your past come to your mind I challenge you to open up your mouth and speak the Word of God to combat that thought because what you say can bring your mind back into alignment. That's why it is important for you to renew your mind with the Word of God. Whatever you allow to go into your mind and stay there will come out of your mouth. *Romans 12:2 says And be not conformed to this world: but be ye transformed by the renewing of your mind, that ye may prove what is that good, and acceptable, and perfect, will of God.*

Let me prove it to you. I want you to count from zero to ten. When you get to the number seven stop counting in your head and say your name out loud you will notice that you had to *stop* thinking in order to say your name out loud.

Death and life is in the power of the tongue. One of most powerful tools to fight against the enemy in your mind is to speak the Word of God into the atmosphere. *Romans 10:17 says so then faith cometh by hearing, and hearing by the word of God.*

I am not suggesting that your mind will never go back to those thoughts after you have declared the Word in the atmosphere. For some of you, after you spoke your name (because you are a focused person) you went back to counting the numbers in your head. The same way that you speak the Word in the atmosphere your mind will still go back to those worldly thoughts. Every time you have a thought, speak the Word, plead the blood of Jesus, and declare that your mind and spirit to come into alignment with the truth, no matter how many times it takes.

THE BOTTOM LINE

You have the power to do this!!!

Let me conclude by reiterating my purpose for writing this book. You do not have to hold an office in the church, carry a title, or be a part of the Fivefold Ministry to deal with an old pattern of demonology. Nor do you have to be afraid of the new devices that the enemy is using. Don't forget the three things that I told you which are:

1. Have faith the size of a mustard seed.
2. Believe that you can be used by God to do it when you operate in the name of Jesus
3. Look for the signs: If you have the previous two then these signs will follow because you believed.

Then as the scripture declares you will be able to cast out devils, you will be able to lay hands on the sick and they shall recover. You will be able to speak with new tongues. You will be able to take up serpents (spiritual warfare) and if you drink any deadly thing it will not hurt you.

Understand God gives us weapons, so now you have to choose the right weapon because no weapon formed against you shall prosper, so no witches, warlocks and black magic, that is formed against you shall prosper either. As well as every tongue that rises in judgment against you shall be condemned which means that the new modern spiritual warfare that rises itself against you, you will have to condemn!

I am comparing the weapons that have been formed against you as the old patterns of witches and warlocks, when God himself forms blocks and prevents them from destroying you. I also compare new modern warfare with the second part of the verse that says every tongue that rises up against you; you shall condemn. In other words the major things that you shall not see God blocks, but things that are visible that we have the power to detach ourselves from or simply cut off we must condemn!

As previously stated let me reinforce the type of power that you really have. Remember John the Baptist was greater than any of the other prophets, but the least of you that would have mustard seed faith is greater than John the Baptist. All those prophets prophesied that Jesus would come. John the Baptist said He is here, however after the cross the Believer can proclaim that HE lives in me.

TOOLS & WEAPONS

To Help You in Battle!

Deal With You

The first tool is you: Those that work for the Army, Navy, Air Force, and Marine know the branches of the armed forces constantly train to always be physically and mentally ready for any challenges that they may face. They are always ready for war. Why are they always ready for war? Because at any moment war can break out! Let's look at the military. The first stage of military training is basic training. You are stripped of your own identity so that you can now take on the identity of whatever military branch you are enlisted. The objective here is to renew and transform your mind so that you can receive the military's new ideas and take on a new way of thinking.

As Believers in the Army of the Lord we have to train in the same manner. We have to first be striped of our identity and take on the new identity of Christ as well as be transformed by the renewing of our minds.

Prepare Physically

Next we have to prepare physically. Let's look at

Matthew 6:16-18 (KJV) 16 Moreover when ye fast, be not, as the hypocrites, of a sad countenance: for they disfigure their faces, that they may appear unto men to fast. Verily I say unto you, They have their reward. 17 But thou, when thou fastest, anoint thine head, and wash thy face; 18 That thou appear not unto men to fast, but unto thy Father which is in secret: and thy Father, which seeth in secret, shall reward thee openly.

Notice the first part of the scripture: *But you, when you fast...*this gives me the impression that fasting is required as a Believer. In my opinion fasting is a basic principle that every Believer should be able to participate in. I also believe that this is a part of our training as Believers. I believe that fasting should be done as the Holy Ghost leads. In addition, consult your doctor before attempting to fast as well.

Next let's look at the next part which is Mark 9:29 (NKJV) *29 So He said to them, "This kind can come out by nothing but prayer and fasting."*

As discussed it will take a combination of belief, fasting, and prayer to defeat the enemy. Again prayer and fasting are the two foundational tools that connect the Believers to God and keeps us forever connected to

God's presence. It is impossible to pray and fast and your belief in God remains smaller than mustard seed faith.

1 Peter 5:8 (NKJV) 8 be sober, be vigilant; because your adversary the devil walks about like a roaring lion, seeking whom he may devour.

Sober: *Abstaining from or habitually abstemious and the use of alcohol drink and other in toxins. Straightforward and serious; not exaggerated, emotional, or silly.*

Vigilant: *Kingly alert to or heedful of trouble or danger as why others are sleeping and unsuspicious. To be kingly watchful to detect trouble; ever awake and alert.*

When you read this scripture along with both definitions. It is clear when our minds are connected to the will of God and not influenced by the imaginations and modern spiritual warfare we would be at a perpetual state of readiness and equipped to defeat the enemy.

Modern Tools

Luke 14:21 so that servant came, and shewed his lord these things. Then the master of the house being angry said to his servant, Go out quickly into the streets and lanes of the city, and bring in hither the poor, and the maimed, and the halt, and the blind. 22 And the servant said, Lord, it is done as thou hast commanded, and yet there is room. 23 And the lord said unto the servant, Go out into the highways and hedges, and compel them to come in, that my house may be filled.

Compel: two force or oblige (someone) to do something. Bring about (something) by the use of force or pressure. (GK) anagkázō – to compel (constrain), doing so with urgency (as a pressing necessity).

We must combat the enemy with modern spiritual warfare tools as well as captivate the people to the point where it forces them to come and experience something different and all that God has to offer for their lives.

So what are some modern tools?

PHONE TOOLS

Married Couples
- There should be transparency in the family as it relates to cell phones.
- Married couples should exchange passwords to keep lines of communication and accountability open and honest.
- Couples should have the ability to answer each other's phone for the same reason as stated above.

Children & Teenagers

Children under the age of 18 years of age:

- Parents should always put some type of parental control on the phone so that you'll know what type of activity is going on with them on the phone. Again the days of looking under the mattresses are not over but we now have to include modern forms of technology to combat the enemy.

- Parents make sure that you are connected to your children on social media and following them so that you can stay informed as to their day-to-day dealings.

- Parents do not allow your children to setup their own social media accounts. It is vital that if you allow them to be to social media you are also the one to control it by having instant access to it.

It is important that there are checks, balances, and open honest communication at all levels of the family, for example your daughter is talking to someone who is thirty years older than her you need to know so that you can put a stop to it. You must be able to combat the devil on his level. You have to step your game up. Modern Spiritual warfare is what's going on right now.

SOCIAL MEDIA

Facebook, Instagram, videos, texting, music, and downloading.

- Social media can be used in a negative way when we are engaged and entertained by it in its various forms. However, it is possible to have control and defeat the enemy when he is using it as a weapon against you.

- One of the things that I would suggest is to be mindful of how you use social media. As humans, we are drawn into lustful things by what we see. It is important to protect your eye gates.

- When you see pictures and images floating down your newsfeed delete them immediately and it may also be a good idea to delete or block the person that posted the pictures and images.

- You want to be careful and protect yourself from anything that is not like God and that will cause you to dive deeper into sinful activities.

- If you have a problem with masturbation it would not be a good idea to keep watching provocative videos of women/ men dancing inappropriately on your Facebook newsfeed or YouTube.

PARENT

- If you are a parent YOU MUST have passwords to all of your kid's social media accounts.

- Their email account is the number one thing that you need access to because in order to have any social media account you must have an email address.

- If you have access to the email you can set it to where every time they get messages inboxes and anything else it will come down your newsfeed.

- Parents also should have access to all cell phone passwords so that you're able to randomly check out what they are viewing and how they are communicating through text messaging.

- This will also give you an opportunity to see how they are using the picture feature on the phone and if they are sending and receiving inappropriate picture and text messages.

- If they are, you warn them that any text, post, pictures and messaging that they send will be out in the world forever unless the other person destroys it. It is these situations that may hurt you in the future if you're dealing with someone who is vindictive.

- Do not post anything on social media that you would not want the world to know about you.

COUPLES

- As safe guard and a check in balance or to hold each other accountable, married couples and or engaged to be married to have the same guidelines as above.

- I would also recommend that when you're making friend request on social media if they are married or that you can clearly see are in a committed relationship it is a good rule of thumb to befriend or request the other person's spouse to let them know that you are legit and there are no issues with you wanting anything inappropriate.

HOW TO HANDLE CONFLICT

- Be careful about telling your personal business on social media. There are certain things that the world does not need to know and if you want to vent to someone out of a negative emotion it is best to contact a family, friend, or a therapist but not to the whole entire world.

- If you have a problem or an issue with someone it is best to call them or inbox them and discuss any issues that you all may have with each other. Remember when you were a child when you and someone argued and the next five minutes you were back on good terms however now in this age of social media it is looked upon childish and you can appear as unstable. Remember the Bible says that a double minded man is unstable in all of his ways. So everything about you will appear to be immature, imbalanced, and unstable causing for people to look at you in negative way when in fact you may not be and acting out based on what could in fact be something normal such as being human however most importantly it could cause future relationships, businesses opportunities, and Kingdom Connections to be missed.

MUSIC

Music has advanced over the years and we now have all forms of music. Any type of music that you want can be downloaded within minutes. Instead of our youth (and some adults) listening to gangster rap or trap music we now have the ability for them to listen to Gospel rap on CD's and/or downloadable.

TELEVISION

As we mentioned previously the Bible teaches that there are things that may not be a sin, however, it is a weight that can easily beset you. Notice the word easily, because these are the things that you like and enjoy watching. When determining if you should allow your mind and spirit to indulge in what you're watching on television at that moment

- Is it God centered and if it is not God centered, is it something that I can learn from that can benefit my life?

- Does this program create an imagination and or desire for people or things that are not in my life currently?

- If left alone would I want my children watching it?

SPIRITUAL TOOLS

Prayer

In order to combat demonic warfare and activity we must use the arsenal of weapons that we as believers have that are available to us. One of those weapons is prayer. Prayer is one the most essential principles of the Christian faith. Prayer allows one to know God and grow spiritually. It is just as important as the air we breathe. If you're feeling as though you're being beaten down and barely alive you may want to check your prayer tank because you may have a leak somewhere.

What is Prayer?

Prayer is the fundamental key to living a successful life. Prayer is as essential to knowing God and growing spiritually as breathing is to living and staying healthy. Prayer is when you actually bring Heaven down to Earth (Matthew 6:10). Prayer gives you the ability to operate in your authority in the spiritual realm. Prayer is vital to your success in every area of your life. Prayer is the way to obtain absolute victory in your life. Prayer is the way to protect every area of your life and it is also the way to defeat the powers darkness. In this section I will outline some basic principles to get you started on your way to a life of victory by defeating the powers of darkness with a lifestyle of prayer.

How do you pray?

Praise: You must speak highly of Him

To get into the presence of the Lord you must first give him praise. Praise is basically giving God applause. It is acclaiming who He is and what He has done! Imagine that you're at a major business conference and the speaker gives an awesome presentation and afterwards the audience gives the speaker a standing ovation and then begins to applaud the speaker to show him or her that they really appreciated him for coming on stage and doing such an amazing job presenting. Psalm 100:4 says, that we must enter into His gates with thanksgiving, and into His courts with praise: be thankful unto him, and bless his name. The Lord our God absolutely loves it when we testify of His goodness and speak highly of Him about the things that He has done for us.

Repent: You must know that you know! Or You Must be a Believer

To defeat the power of the enemy you must know that you know that you are a child of God. One of the ways that the enemy defeats the people of God is that he leads them to believe they are not forgiven and could not possibly be a child of God. The bible declares in Romans 10:9 that if you confess with your mouth the Lord Jesus and believe in your heart that God has raised Him from the dead, you will be saved. Point blank period! You can take that to the bank! As a born again Believer and child of the King there are certain rights that come with that Kingship! The operative word here is "Believer". I believe that it is possible to follow Christ and not be a Believer in Christ. Being a Christian is not enough you must be a believer. Judas Iscariot followed Jesus and but did not truly believe in Jesus. Thomas followed Jesus but did not fully believe in Him. The bible says in Mark 16:17-18 that if you are a Believer in His name (Jesus) shall they cast out devils; they shall speak with new tongues; they shall take up serpents; and if they drink any deadly thing, it shall not hurt them; they shall lay hands on the sick, and they shall recover. These are all things that you will need in order to assist in your pursuit to defeat the enemy.

You must never doubt your salvation or believe any of the deceitful ways that the enemy tries to use to convince you that you're not a child of the Most High! Yes you're going to mess up along your journey with the Lord. You're even going to make a few mistakes; to be honest it will be more than a few mistakes but listen making a mistake does not make you lose your place in God. You may fall out of the will of God but you must know that you know that you're still in His plan. So I will say to you that when you fall short repent quickly which means to ask for forgiveness and turn away from your sins. Move on don't dwell in the land of defeat and not enough! You have to remember that God is omniscience, which means that He knows all. If He knows all than surely He knew what your mistakes will and would be before you made them. So again repent be of good cheer because your sins are forgiven, if you asked Him to forgive and if you believe that He did.

Adoration: We must worship Him

Next we must adore Him! Adoration is basically worshipping God. As His creation, we must show a deep love and respect for Him. When we worship the Lord our God Jesus Christ He will handle any of our troubles because He does not want anything to come between us worshipping Him. We were created to Worship our God. Adoration or worship is different than praise. Worship is where we honor God for who he is and not for what He has done and that my friend is the difference between the two. When we know the difference we can truly honor God appropriately!

Don't Be Afraid To Ask God Questions

As a child I would hear adults often say, "Don't question God". As a child I never fully understood the purpose for such logic. As we stated before Our God is a God that knows everything. And if He knows everything then why am I walking around trying to guest on questions that only He has the answers too? When your God knows everything you don't have to wonder, guest, or get second hand information that may or may not work. As a matter of fact you can go directly to the source to get all of the answers that you need. The bible declares in Luke 11:9 says that if we as believers ask it will be given, seek, and we shall find, and knock and it shall be opened unto us. This scripture indicates that every time we "ask God" he will respond to us with an answer. We may have to wait for His answer but rest assured he will answer and the response will be well worth the wait.

Don't be afraid to ask your Father for what you need and for the things that concern you and your family. Unload all of your Burdens and cares on Him. He care so much for you that He will sustain you and never allow you to be shaken as long as you're in right standing with Him.

Speak "the Word":

There are times where we must ask God in order for things to happen in our lives, our loved ones lives, and in the lives of those that we come into contact with however there will come a time in which you will have to ask no questions but instead DECLARE the Word of the Lord! One of the biggest lies and tactics that the enemy uses is isolation and loneliness. He wants us to believe that we are on an island and in this war alone and by ourselves. The very moment that you feel this way you must stand tall and speak the Word of God by using every scripture that refutes every lie that satan tries to tell you about your situation and circumstances. When you're operating to the fullness of who you are in God when you speak the Word of God and people hear you they are hearing Jesus speak because you are His representative in the Earth! Go ahead use your authority and speak the Word! When we use God's word we gain access to His power!

Know "the Word":

In order to know what parts of the Word to speak you need to know the Word. The bible states in 2 Timothy 2:15 that we must become students of the word of God by studying to show thyself approved. One of the basic principles of a disciple or student of God is to study the Word, Apply it to your life, and reap the promises. How do you know the promises if you do not study? How do you know what you're rights are if you don't study. How do you know how to combat the enemy if you're not a student of the Word of God? Where does your strength come from if your do not study the Word? The Word of God is a weapon in the arsenal for modern spiritual warfare against the enemy.

How often do you pray?

Prayer should be an extremely important and significant part of your life. It is not something that is done at church alone or when you're with other Believers of Christ. Prayer is a daily discipline for Believers. You must be consistently faithful in your prayer life in order to have optimum success in every area of your life. The bible declares that we are to always pray! Specifically in Ephesians 6:18 "Praying always with all prayer and supplication in the Spirit, and watching thereunto with all perseverance and supplication for all saints." This scripture is basically interpreted as saying: Pray anytime and every time there's an opportunity to pray; no matter where you are, what you're doing, or whom you're with. Use every occasion, season, situation, and every possible moment to pray. Praying is nonnegotiable but the logistics of praying is variable for example where or if you're standing or listening to music etc. Believers of Jesus Christ should make prayer a priority!

Meditation

You have given God Praise for what He has done. You have Worshipped Him for who He is. You've repented for any sins and shortcomings. You've spoken the Word and studied it as well. You've even been faithful and consistent in your prayer life. Now you've come to the point where it is time to enjoy His presence or what I call meditation!

What is Meditation?

The next weapon that you have in your arsenal for combat is Meditation. In my opinion meditation is where you have an opportunity to enjoy the presence of God! Meditation is that quality time that you spend with him listening to what He has to say. I believe that Praying is when you talk to God but Meditation is when He talks to you! Believers should take time to meditate on God's Word and what he is saying to us as we move forward into the things that He has called us to. Meditation is where God will at times answer some of our questions that we have asked. Meditation is where He may choose to give us a breakthrough idea to implement. Meditation is that quiet time with God. There are approximately 27 verses in the bible that speak on meditation. The scripture tells us in *Psalm 1:1-3* that a blessed man delights in the Law (Word) of the Lord and in that Law (Word) he mediates day and night and that if he does so he will be strong as a tree that stands firm by the water that will not go anywhere but he will reap fruit when it time to reap. Meditating on the word of God will cause you to maintain your stamina and spiritual beauty.

Remember in the book of *Joshua 1:8* The Lord God tells Joshua to not only speak the Word but to meditate on the word day and night, so that he can have a lifestyle that holds up the standard of everything that God told them to do which will in return make Joshua's way prosperous and successful.

Also take into account that in Genesis 24:63 when Isaac went out to mediate on the fields one evening and he looked up and camels were coming! Yes Meditation will cause increase and blessings to come to you! Meditation is a massive weapon in the arsenal because it gives you the insight that you need in order to have success in warfare!

FASTING

What is fasting?

Fasting is basically abstaining or reducing certain or all food, drink, or both, for a certain period of time. There is also what is known as an absolute fast, which is normally, defined as abstinence from all food and liquid for a certain period, usually a period of 24 hours, or a number of days.

Fasting can be defined in many ways however we find in today's church or mindset the belief that fasting is anything that you give up for a certain amount of time is considered fasting however according to the bible fasting must be a restraining from food.

What is the purpose of fasting?

The purpose of fasting is to deny your flesh of the things that it craves in order to tune out the distractions of the world so that you can to hear from God

Being that we live in a modern time period and there are other things that we can refrain from as well. For instance there are some people that fast from social media, phones, television, going out to the movies and social events.

Fasting is that one thing that many believers including myself do not like to do. Fasting usually takes an act of heaven to move in one spirit for them to submit yourself to this powerful tool. Fasting along with prayer has the ability to do several things. Fasting disciplines the spirit, mind, and body. When a person truly fast and meditate on God and His word they will find that their life will become more disciplined as well as desires & temptations become less. You will find yourself being more spiritual minded rather than being carnal.

Notice Jesus Christ after being baptized the first thing that he does he goes in the wilderness for fast for 40 days. It is clear to me that Jesus set fasting as a pattern for us to follow before true ministry.

Now there are some disclaimers you need to understand about fasting. When Jesus came out of the wilderness after the His 40 day fast the first thing the devil tempted Him with was food.

Matthew 4:1-4 (KJV)

4 Then was Jesus led up of the Spirit into the wilderness to be tempted of the devil. 2 And when he had fasted forty days and forty nights, he was afterward hungered. 3 And when the tempter came to him, he said, If thou be the Son of God, command that these stones be made bread. 4 But he answered and said, It is written, Man shall not live by bread alone, but by every word that proceedeth out of the mouth of God.

The devil dared Jesus to turn stones into bread. The first thing that I noticed is that the enemy questioned Jesus's divinity and tried to take Jesus out of position by presenting with the very thing that he knew Jesus wanted. Jesus did not give in to the temptation that he was presented with because he knew exactly who he was and did not have to prove it to anyone. Jesus knew that His assignment was great and he was not going to allow something as simple as food to take him out of position. Understand that when you fast and the devil knows that you mean it he will send the various things that you are trying to sustain from to your presence. Fasting will cause hunger pains but when one has made up their mind to get what they need from God they will take these pains as an indication to go further and pray harder.

Fasting doesn't always change your situation immediately but it changes your mindset to stand in front of whatever demonic force that is front of you.

Notice what Esther does, she sends a decree for Mordecai for him and his people to fast for her. While she and her people fasted where they were. After fasting she said I am going to see the King, if I perish let me perish. Notice what happens before she gets an answer from the king her mindset about her life and its position immediately changes. Fasting will prepare you for a greater life or it will prepare you for a Victorious death which will give glory to the Lord.

Esther 4:14-16King James Version (KJV)

14 For if thou altogether holdest thy peace at this time, then shall there enlargement and deliverance arise to the Jews from another place; but thou and thy father's house shall be destroyed: and who knoweth whether thou art come to the kingdom for such a time as this? 15 Then Esther bade them return Mordecai this answer, 16 Go, gather together all the Jews that are present in Shushan, and fast ye for me, and neither eat nor drink three days, night or day: I also and my maidens will fast likewise; and so will I go in unto the king, which is not according to the law: and if I perish, I perish.

Let's take a look at the children of Nineveh. God had made a decree that they would die, that their sins had come up before him. The king ordered everyone including the animals on a fast. The Bible records after prayer and fasting that God, keyword God Himself repented of the evil that he had said that He would do unto Him and He did it not. So we see the power of fasting can change God's mind, shift a nation, and surely it can change your life.

Lastly, when fasting, don't be like the Pharisee's did in biblical times, fasting and praying for attention. Maintain your hygiene, keep your face washed, clothes clean, and do not broadcast your fast. If you're invited to dinner just say "maybe another time". There is no need to mention anything about your fast doing so will possibly become your reward.

Matthew 6:4 (KJV)

4 That thine alms may be in secret: and thy Father which seeth in secret himself shall reward thee openly.

When you fast and consecrate your body to God it is an indication to Him that you want to worship Him in a Greater way. Remember that your body is the temple of the living God just like your home. Every now and then there must be a spring-cleaning in order to clean out what's inside. This is what fasting does it prepares your body temple to be filled and used by God.

Modern spiritual warfare is having the ability to look at the enemy and calculate how you're going to offset him. We must fight iron with iron, fire with fire. We must operate in spiritual warfare in a modern way using the same cutting tools, technology, and weapons that the enemy uses against us. This is one time that I believe that we should operate the same as trained law enforcement officers, not with just equal force but with every appropriate force it takes to subdue, and arrest every demonic force that has been sent on assignment from the wicked places of darkness. We do not show up to a gun, battle with a knife, nor do we run around looking and operating from an old pattern of spiritual warfare. We will be as Nehemiah when he built the wall. We will work with one hand while holding a weapon in the other. We will watch as well as pray. We will be ye also ready. We will have the amount of artillery that is needed no more and no less.

We have a responsibility to be both spiritual and aware as well as take heed to the devices of the enemy so that we can combat him with the appropriate measure of force. We don't ask, we take we don't bargain, we demand. And it is in this manner that we use Modern Spiritual Warfare Tools to Take the World by Force!!!!!!

Daily Warfare Prayer
Apostle Edith Moore

Satan! It is written! Greater is HE (JESUS) who is in us than you who are in the world. On this basis, you and your cohorts are already defeated. Your final destination is the horrendous 'Lake of Fire'; the weapons of our warfare are mighty - in God, for the pulling down of your strongholds.

Therefore: Satan, we bind you in the name of Jesus. Strongman over (Your county), we bind you in the name of Jesus. Strongman over (Your County), we bind you in the name of Jesus.

And we bind your strongholds of: sexual immorality (impurity, promiscuity, adultery, lust), idolatry, witchcraft, hatred (racial discrimination) rivalry, jealously, anger, quarrels, conflicts, division, envy, murder, alcohol and drug abuse, wild partying, laziness, poverty, hopelessness, depression, greed, revenge, vanity, envy, sloth, gluttony and illness.

We bring every thought captive to the obedience of Jesus Christ and according to the word loose: Reconciliation (gospel of peace) love, joy, peace, patience, kindness, goodness, faithfulness, gentleness, self-control, excellent health - long life, prosperity (through hard work) and every good gift that comes from above." **In Jesus' precious name, Amen.**

ABOUT THE AUTHOR

Christopher A. Moore is the Chief Prelate of Emmanuel Covenant Community Churches and Pastor of Emmanuel Empowerment Temple in Kingsland, Ga. He recently opened a second location, Emmanuel Outreach Campus, in Brunswick, Ga., which focuses on going out into the city to reach all souls. At the age of fourteen, he was ordained as a minister under Bishop Thomas Weeks. He holds a Bachelor's Degree in Theology, a Master's Degree in Divinity, and a Doctorate Degree in Christian Education (PhD).

God has blessed Overseer Moore to serve under many great leaders such as Bishop Thomas Weeks (Pentecostal Assemblies of the World), Bishop Levi Willis Jr. (Church of God in Christ), Bishop Joseph Showell (Bible Way), the late Bishop David L. Ellis (Pentecostal Assemblies of the World) and Apostle Edith Moore (Emmanuel Ministries Worldwide, Inc.), Pastor G. Bobby Hall (Church of God in Christ). Overseer Moore sits on the Board of Bishops and Overseers for Emmanuel Ministries Worldwide, Inc., churches in Georgia, Florida, the Bahamas and Africa. He has the ability to preach to both, scholars and babes in Christ by infusing theology with practical life principles, which produces a word that touches all walks of life and spiritual levels. He is known for his relevant, dynamic, and illustrative preaching and ability to bring God's word to life through his sermons.

Overseer Christopher Moore has a heart for his local community. He started the Standing His Ground Unity Movement in efforts to unite the community across racial, class, and social boundaries. He is employed as a Chaplain at UF Hospital (Shands) in Jacksonville, Florida as well as Deputy & Chaplain for the Camden County Sheriff's Office and Camden County High school football team. He also currently serves as Chairman of the Board for United Way of Camden County, Ga. He continues to be an advocate of the word of God, having a genuine love for people. His motto is "NEVER REST UNTIL YOUR GOOD IS BETTER AND YOUR BETTER IS BEST".

www.ingramcontent.com/pod-product-compliance
Lightning Source LLC
LaVergne TN
LVHW051812080426
835513LV00017B/1928